Food Zone

All About Vegetables

Vic Parker

QEB Publishing

Published in the United States by
QEB Publishing, Inc.
3 Wrigley, Suite A
Irvine, CA 92618

www.qeb-publishing.com

Library of Congress Cataloging-in-Publication Data

Parker, Victoria.
 All about vegetables / Vic Parker.
      p. cm. -- (QEB food zone)
Includes index.
ISBN 978-1-59566-771-7 (hardcover)
1. Vegetables--Juvenile literature. I. Title.
TX401.P35 2010
 641.3'5--dc22

2008056075

Printed and bound in China

Words in **bold** are explained
in the glossary on page 22.

Author Vic Parker
Consultant Angela Royston
Project Editor Eve Marleau
Designer Kim Hall
Illustrator Mike Byrne

Publisher Steve Evans
Creative Director Zeta Davies
Managing Editor Amanda Askew

Picture credits
(t=top, b=bottom, l=left, r=right, c=center, fc=front
cover)

Alamy Images 12c Agripicture Images/Peter Dean,
13cl Itani, 14cl David Chilvers,
14cr Mark Saunders, 15t Cultura/Bill Sykes,
18cr Nigel Cattlin
Corbis 4br Fancy/Veer
Dreamstime 11bl (babycorn) Andy St John
FLPA 19t Nigel Cattlin
Getty Images 15cl Iconica/Andersen Ross
Photolibrary 9t Fresh Food Images/Tim Hill,
12b Botanica, 13t Chris L Jones, 15cr Johner/Anna
Skoog, 19cl Foodpix/Gottlieb Dennis,
19b Foodpix/Ann Stratton
Shutterstock 4tl Andrjuss, 4tr Lepas, 4cl Yellowj, 4cr
Mashe, 4bl Elena Schweitzer,
4-5 Elnur, 5t WitR, 5bl S.Fierros, 5bc Norma Cornes,
5br Filipe B. Varela, 6 Lepas, 7tl Mashe, 7tr Sergey
Kolodkin, 7c Andrjuss, 7bl Harris Shiffman, 7br
Yellowj, 8t Alena Ozerova,
8bl Joe Gough, 8bc Thomas M Perkins,
8br Khz, 9b Luchschen, 11t Sandra Caldwell,
11c (carrots) Mashe, 11c (sweetcorn) Sandra
Caldwell, 11bl (broccoli) Andrjuss, 11bcl (half
zucchini) PhotoPips, 11bcr (beetroot) Sergey
Kolodkin, 11br (pepper) Paul Cowan, 12t Yellowj, 13bl
Harris Shiffman, 13br Lepas, 13cr Leonid Shcheglov,
14t Mashe, 14b Christopher
Halloran, 15b Sandra Caldwell, 16 Lepas,
17l Elena Schweitzer, 17r Sandra Caldwell,
18t Andrjuss, 18cl Rafa Fabrykiewicz,
18b Oxana Zuboff, 19cr Angela Hawkey

Contents

What are vegetables?

Vegetables are parts of plants that you can eat.

There are many different kinds of vegetables, such as potatoes, peas, carrots, and zucchini.

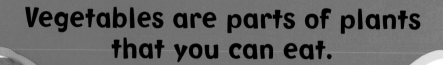

Potatoes

Zucchini

Peas

Carrots

Vegetable plants come in many shapes and sizes. Lettuces and cabbages are round and leafy.

Cabbage

Lettuce

4

You will need
. . . .

- An empty eggshell
- Some cotton wool
- Felt-tip pens
- Cress seeds
- Egg cup
- Water

Grow a... cress plant

1 Fill half of the large part of an empty eggshell with cotton wool.

2 Put your shell in an egg cup and draw a funny face on it with felt-tip pens.

3 Pour some water on the cotton wool until it is very wet and sprinkle some cress seeds onto it.

4 Water your seeds every day and wait for your egg's "hair" to sprout.

Leeks are straight and tall.
The part of onions and beetroot
that you eat grows underground.

Leek

Beetroot

Onion

Where are vegetables grown?

Different vegetables are grown all over the world.

They need the right conditions in order to grow. Some vegetables need lots of light and little water. They grow best in hot countries.

Some vegetables need lots of water. They grow best in countries where there is plenty of rain.

North America

South America

Zucchini are grown in warm parts of North America.

Carrots are grown around the UK.

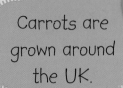

Beetroot grows well in cool, damp weather. It is often farmed in Eastern Europe.

Europe

Asia

Potatoes are the most popular vegetable to eat in Australia. They are the most widely grown vegetable in the world.

Africa

Oceania

Okra is eaten in stews, soups, and curries. It grows well in hot, dry places, such as Africa and the Caribbean.

A lot of peas are grown in Greece and Turkey, where they are then added to soups and stews.

7

How do we eat vegetables?

Vegetables can be eaten raw or cooked at any time of day.

For lunch, you might eat raw vegetables in a salad or have a Russian beetroot soup called borscht.

At breakfast, you might eat a mushroom **omelet**.

For dinner, you might have a Chinese vegetable stir fry—or eat vegetables with a portion of meat, chicken, or fish.

8

Some people never eat meat, chicken, or fish. These people are vegetarian. In countries such as India, many people add spices to their cooking to make vegetable dishes tasty.

⇧ Cauliflower is a vegetable that is often used in Indian cooking.

You will need

- 1 large pizza base
- 2 tbsp of tomato paste
- 1 onion, sliced
- 5 large mushrooms, sliced
- 1 red pepper, sliced
- 5 oz/150 g grated cheese
- Baking tray

Make a... vegetable pizza

1 Ask an adult to set the oven to 400°F/200°C/Gas 6.

2 Spread the tomato paste across the pizza base.

3 Arrange the sliced vegetables on top. Sprinkle with the cheese.

4 Ask an adult to put your pizza on the baking tray and bake in the oven for 10–15 minutes, until the cheese turns golden brown.

Why does your body need vegetables?

Vegetables are packed with vitamins and minerals that are good for your body.

Vegetables such as broccoli contain iron, which keeps your **nervous system** and blood healthy.

Vegetables such as cauliflower contain **fiber**, which helps your body to get rid of waste food.

Carrots contain vitamin C, which helps to protect the body from illnesses. It is also needed for your body to **absorb** the mineral iron from your food.

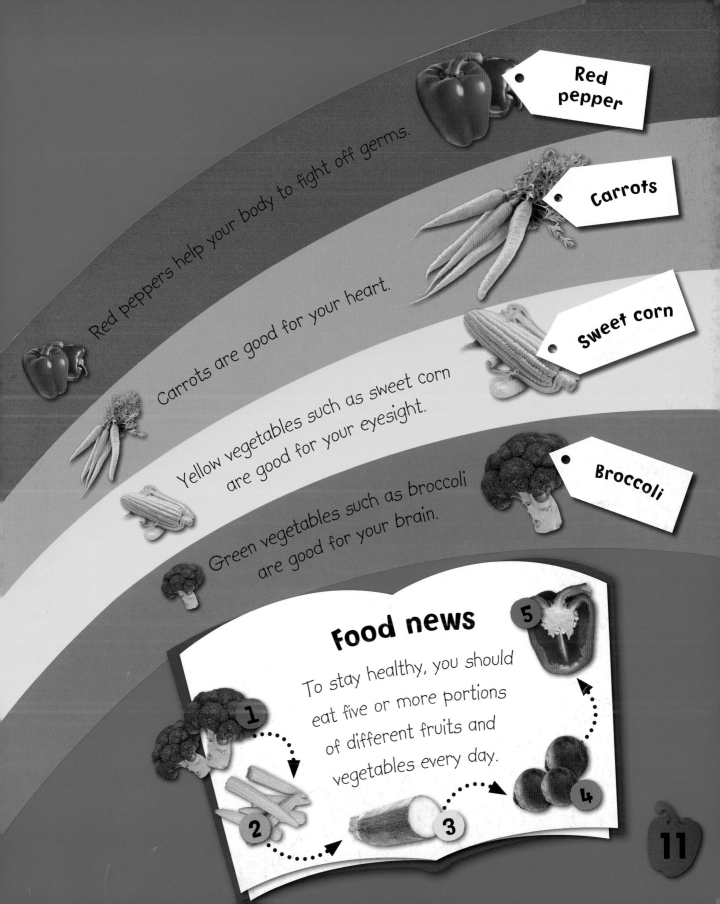

Red peppers help your body to fight off germs.

Red pepper

Carrots are good for your heart.

Carrots

Yellow vegetables such as sweet corn are good for your eyesight.

Sweet corn

Green vegetables such as broccoli are good for your brain.

Broccoli

Food news

To stay healthy, you should eat five or more portions of different fruits and vegetables every day.

1 2 3 4 5

Peas

How are peas grown?

Peas grow well in soil that has lots of compost **added so it is full of goodness.**

1 Pea seeds can be sown, or planted, from March to June, straight into rows in soil.

Pea plants must be watered often. Peas in **pods** can be quite heavy, so the plants need to be tied onto canes or nets for support as they grow.

2

3 After about nine weeks, flowers appear. The seeds inside the flowers swell and become peas.

Around three weeks later, the peas are ready to **harvest**. Pea farmers have special machines that pull the pea plants out of the ground.

4

5 Some peas are sent straight to stores. Most are stripped from their pods and then canned or frozen.

Eat a... raw pea

Open a fresh pea pod and squeeze out the peas—they are super-sweet and tasty.

How are carrots grown?

Carrots grow well in soil that has no weeds.

1 Carrot seeds can be sown, or planted any time from the middle of February to July.

Seedlings start to appear just 15–20 days after planting.

2

3 Carrots grow underground, so all you can see are their green, leafy tops.

Carrots

14

4 When the leafy tops start to **wilt**, the vegetables are ready for harvesting. This is any time from June to October.

Farmers have special machines that pick carrots from the ground.

5

6 Many carrots are taken to stores and sold fresh. Some are canned or frozen.

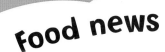

Food news

If a carrot top is placed in a saucer of water, it will begin to sprout new leaves after a few days.

15

Zucchini

Grow some zucchini

Zucchini seeds should be sown, or planted, between March and the end of May.

1

Push the seed into the small pot on its side. Water it and leave the pot inside near sunlight.

2

When roots show through the bottom of the pot, replant it in your medium pot. Water the plant and leave outside if it is warm.

3

After two months, carefully turn your zucchini plant out of the medium pot and replant it in the bucket.

Wait until your zucchini are about 4 inches (10 centimeters) long, then pick them. For a few weeks, more zucchini will continue to grow, so keep watering your plant every day.

4

Eat a... zucchini flower

Chop a zucchini flower into a salad or add it to a pasta dish.

Potatoes

How are potatoes grown?

Potatoes grow well in sunny places.

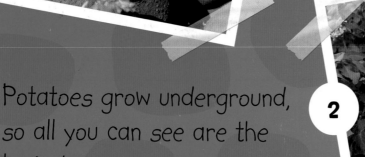

1 Old potatoes have buds, or "eyes". If they are planted in spring, they grow shoots.

Potatoes grow underground, so all you can see are the leafy tops.

2

3 The tops of the plants turn yellow after several weeks. It is now time to harvest the potatoes. This happens from early summer to late fall.

4 Each plant produces several potatoes. Farmers use a special machine to pull the potatoes from the ground.

Most potatoes go straight to stores to be sold fresh. Some go to factories where they are turned into foods such as fries or chips.

5

King Edward

Maris Piper

Food news

There are thousands of types of potatoes. They have names such as King Edward, Maris Piper, Desiree, and Rooster. They all look and taste slightly different.

Rooster

Desiree

Make zucchini boats

Try using zucchini to make this tasty and healthy dish.

You will need

- 2 tbsp of vegetable oil
- 2 large zucchini
- 1 onion, finely chopped
- 6 tomatoes, finely chopped
- 3 small mushrooms, chopped
- 2 garlic cloves, finely chopped
- 2 tbsp of breadcrumbs
- 2 tbsp of parmesan, grated
- Salt and pepper
- Knife
- Teaspoon
- Frying pan
- Wooden spoon
- Small mixing bowl
- Greased baking dish

1

Preheat the oven to 350°F/180°C/Gas 6. Cut the zucchini in half. Scoop out the insides and keep it.

2

Ask an adult to lightly fry the onions and garlic in oil until they begin to soften.

3 Add the zucchini flesh, mushrooms, tomatoes, and a pinch of salt and pepper. Fry for five more minutes.

Mix the breadcrumbs and grated cheese together.

4

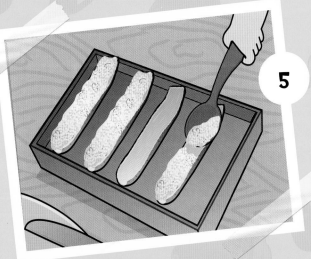

5 Put your zucchini boats in the baking dish. Fill them with the vegetables, then add the breadcrumb and cheese mixture on top.

Ask an adult to put them in the oven for 30 minutes. Serve straight away.

6

Glossary

Absorb
To take something in.

Compost
Rotting plant material that is full of goodness. It is added to soil to improve its quality.

Fiber
A part of plants that your body can't digest. As fiber moves through your body, it soaks up water and makes it easier to get rid of waste food.

Harvest
To gather, or collect, crops from the field.

Nervous system
The main system in control of your body, made up of your brain and a network of nerves.

Omelet
A meal made by beating an egg and then frying it. Other ingredients, such as mushrooms, ham, and cheese, are often added.

Pod
The long, flat part of a pea plant that contains the peas.

Wilt
When a plant wilts, it bends over because it is too old or dry.

Notes for parents and teachers

- Show the children a variety of food and pick out the fresh vegetables. Discuss each vegetable's size, shape, color, and texture.

- Explain the conditions each vegetable needs to grow and talk about where each vegetable grows in the world. Look at a map or globe to identify the places where each vegetable comes from.

- Find photographs of what different vegetables look like when they are growing. Choose one to draw and then label the different parts of the plant (roots, stem, branches, leaves, and fruit).

- Discuss which vegetables we can eat raw and which we need to cook. Talk about which parts of the vegetable we can eat and which parts we should throw away. Show other forms that the vegetable comes in, such as tinned and frozen.

- Discuss why our bodies need vegetables to stay healthy. Explain how many vegetables we should eat each day and why it's best to eat different kinds.

- Talk about how we might use different types of vegetables in cooking. Make an international vegetable cookbook with recipes and pictures from around the world.

Index